Everybody's Everybody

A children's musical about hunger in the world

and

a fundraiser for famine
because
Everybody can help

by Merrill Collins
and Frederick Gums

Dedication

"Everybody's Everybody"
is dedicated
to serving the needs
of hungry children in Africa,
and offering children who wish to help
an educational, creative and
enjoyable way to participate
in service to the world community.

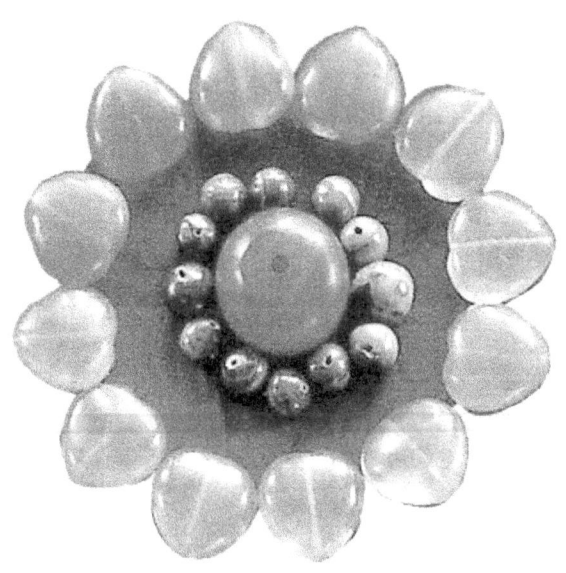

"Any child who needs you could be the
child who leads you to that place, where
Everybody's Everybody"

INTRODUCTION

100 years ago, before there was a United Nations (1942) or the Universal Declaration of Human Rights (1948), the League of Nations adopted the Geneva Declaration on the Rights of the Child, which basically stated that humanity "owes to the Child the best that it has to give." This 1924 declaration articulates that children need priority, protection, and a dignified upbringing. The UN adopted this declaration in 1959, but the idea got real teeth in 1989, when it became the Convention on the Rights of the Child, a convention being different from a declaration in that it moves from being an *ideal* to being the *law*. For the past 35 years now, the world has begun the process of making sure children are legally protected everywhere in the world.

There are 41 rights listed in the CRC, many of them (like the right to identity, nationality, and freedom from discrimination) echoing the UDHR. Some of them are very specific to children, such as Article 27, which states that children have the right to food, clothing and a safe home. Articles 12 and 13 that say children have the right to express their views. Article 42 states that everyone needs to know what the rights of children are.

Author and composer Merrill Collins took these mandates to heart when she and her collaborator, Fredrick Gums, who were running an arts program for kids to teach concepts in Peace, created this poignant children's musical. They wrote it with children, in the voices of children, for audiences of children, all of whom are trying to understand this grownup world and problems like poverty and hunger. And they wrote it as a fundraiser to help children who were experiencing famine. The brilliance of this co-creation is, to quote actor Jeff Bridges, that "poverty is a very complicated issue, but hunger isn't." It empowers every single person involved in the production to help raise awareness, and raise money, and simply send food to those who need it.

The musical is beautiful. The staging is imaginative. Best of all, Merrill's passion for educating communities about key world agreements through music is infectious. This guide provides detailed instructions that make the production simple and strong, including activities to engage children about The Rights of Children, and impactful information to provide during intermission. When children understand Children's Rights, they become humans who understand Human Rights. And as we move forward on this magnificent project of creating a world where everyone has dignity, the planet becomes a more respectful, safe, optimistic, and beautiful place where "everybody's everybody."

—Kristen Caven, playwright and
co-author of *The Bullying Antidote* and
The Winning Family: Where No One Has to Lose,
Summer 2024

A Local/Global Community Service Project

Everybody's Everybody is intended to educate children and the general public about
problems children face on the globe, how we can respond by reaching out,
and monies collected from ticket sales are to be delivered
by the children to a chosen charity.

*Chris Ray at age six, 1985, presenting a check to
Buster of KRON4 of monies raised from ticket
sales for "Airlift to Africa."*

CONTENTS

Introduction by Kristen Caven iii

Composer's Notes 1
Cast 3
Synopsis 4
Casting the Adult Support Team 7
Preparing the Play 8

Script 11

Scores (lead sheets only) 29
    Help Them Live
    Dream Show
    Hunger
    Neglect
    Dream Show (reprise)
    Poverty
    Everybody's Everybody
    We're Calling You
    We Can Make a Difference

Appendicies 41
Notes for Music Educators 43
How to Use the Audio Soundtrack 44
Resources 45
About the Artists 46

For more information on producing this musical benefit,
please contact the publisher.
www.spiralingmusic.com

History Of This Musical

Everybody's Everybody was originally developed in 1985 at a YMCA after school performing arts program in Oakland, California. Frederick Gums was the director, and had established a program called "Social Awareness Via The Arts". The curricula goal plan for the year was:

September-October:	· Develop community within the group
November-December:	· Extend activities to reach into the immediate neighborhood and town; build understanding of community
January-May:	· Create a local / global service project connecting to the larger world community.

At that time, my son Chris Ray was one of fifty children who attended daily. He was then six years old. I was bartering my services as a professional musician in exchange for his tuition. Frederick wanted to work with the children to write a musical drama addressing the Ethiopian famine. News of the famine had reached all of us through major media. All of us were impacted by photo images of emaciated children, shown on T.V., in magazines and newspapers. The images were evoking a world wide humanitarian response. As we developed this project, the intention was to offer the children a way of participating creatively and constructively in what was a global crises.

Frederick designed art projects for the children, which included home-made costumes and set design. The hunger monster was large, with sixteen little feet. All of the children planned and constructed their own tropical fish costume for the Neglect scene. A child's illustration of a fish tank was selected, photographed, and projected as the scenery. All together, they constructed a very large cylindrical object which was then painted to become an oversized can of fish food. With a cast of fifty, (the entire enrollment) and only a dozen leading roles, we included all of the children in the chorus and fish dance, ending Act I. The final chorus of Everybody's Everybody, through to the finale, featured the whole group.

For the multi-media presentation, Poverty, we were fortunate to find a local newspaper journalist who offered documentary photo slides of children in Ethiopia. Frederick photographed the children at the Oakland site, and we alternated the images of the Oakland children and the Ethiopian children as the pre-recorded interviews were played through the sound system. A local sound engineer volunteered time and equipment to record and edit the interviews prepared for the Poverty scene.

As the service project got going many skilled professional people volunteered their support. My band at the time, the "Spirit of the Occasion Ensemble" provided live music. Many parents also participated, making the effort a successful expression of inter-generational activism.

KRON4 T.V. Community Affairs in San Francisco was featuring a fund-raising drive, "Airlift to Africa". I contacted the department, described the Everybody's Everybody musical, and director Javier Valencia decided to send a camera crew over to the site. The children sang "Help Them Live", which became a public service announcement shown on the evening news in conjunction with the "Airlift". Later that year when the entire show was performed, ticket sales raised $750 which the children hand delivered to the T.V. station as an additional contribution.

Everybody's Everybody, 2005

A lot has progressed since 1985 when this musical was first written. The key concepts of the project can still apply, with a few adjustable factors being added. The concepts are:

- a) Humanitarian responses to help children in need are natural and can lead into appropriate action.
- b) Young children often feel these responses when seeing or hearing about the plights of other children.
- c) Adults can guide children into participation with organizations that serve others.
- d) Participation in service helps build self-esteem among children.
- e) Service projects help build stronger communities, locally as well as globally.

The Convention on the Rights of the Child came into being 1989-1990, and works well as an educational tool in conjunction with the project. This document can assist youth in understanding the international community's relationship and commitment to the needs of children.

Adjustable Factors, Who to Serve?

In revising the materials, the specific references to Ethiopia have been re-written to indicate "a foreign country", which can be selected individually by whatever group of children is doing the project. The project director works with the group, choosing how to set up the benefit to serve selected recipients in Africa.

Recently the crises in Darfur, Africa has necessitated humanitarian response. Chris Ray is now twenty five years old. He said that of all the projects we did when he was young, one of the best he remembered was "Everybody's Everybody". Famines are still going on. Malnutrition among children is still a world wide concern. So we decided to revive the musical and record the sound track. In reviving Everybody's Everybody, the intention is to put forward the materials, script, scores, audio soundtrack, to make this valuable project available.

Acknowledgements

My gratitude is heart felt for all who participated in Everybody's Everybody in the past and to all who choose to bring these themes to life in the current time.

May the benefits reach many!

Merrill Collins

June 2005

EVERYBODY'S EVERYBODY

CAST OF CHARACTERS

Children # 1-8
   Eight children play the leading roles in scenes 1,2,3, and then become the "Dream Kids" In the original production, the children kept their real names. For identification in the script, numbers have been used, however it is suggested that the children #1-8 be called their true names in the production.

A Television Newsroom Announcer

Mom #1

A Dad

A Radio Announcer

Mom #2

Fact reporters #1, #2, #3

Dream Show Host

Hunger Monster (8 Children)

Fish #1, #2, #3, #4

Chorus

Dancers

EVERYBODY'S EVERYBODY

Synopsis

ACT I:

Scene 1

Three children are at home in the evening watching TV in their living room.
The news report coverage is about hungry children facing famine in a foreign country.
The youngest child asks questions. The older children answer, however none of them really understand the "WHY" of the topic, and so they call a question to their mother who is offstage. The mother has no answer, and tells the children it is their bedtime.

Scene 2

Four children and their father are in a living room in their home. The father sits in a chair reading a newspaper. The children sit on the floor on a rug, reading magazines and looking at photographs of starving children. The children speak to their dad about wanting to go and give the hungry children some food. Their dad says the hungry children are too far away. The children talk about a space shuttle as they prepare for bedtime.

Scene 3

One child is in his bedroom dancing to music being played on his boom box. A news flash comes on the radio and reveals statistics about how many children died that day from the famine. The child listening goes to the other room to tell his mother. His mother reminds him it is bedtime.

Scene 4

The lights go down and the children from scenes 1, 2, and 3 go to the next scene where they are all together in the same dream. While they are in transit to the dream, the chorus sings, along with the children playing leading roles, the song: "Help Them Live". While the lights are down, during the instrumental bridge of the song, a spotlight appears on three different children, one at a time, standing on the side of the stage. The first two are "fact reporters" and speak facts about children in a foreign country in need. The third reporter reads an article from the Convention on the Rights of the Child.

Scene 5

The lights come up and the children who are now together in the same dream (now called the Dream Kids) are greeted by the Dream Show Host, who sings the song: "Dream Show". The goal of the game is to ask the right question. The song ends abruptly as the Hunger Monster runs out onto the stage. The Hunger Monster sings the song "Hunger" and scares the Dream Kids, who later band together to confront the Monster, singing the last lines of "Help Them Live". The Monster backs away. The Dream Show Host congratulates the Dream Kids, who have won a prize by asking the right question. He announces their prize: An old fish tank filled with hungry fish and an added bonus prize of a large can of fish food.

Scene 6

A large fish tank is the backdrop of this scene. Next to the tank stands a very large can of fish food. The Dream Kids sit on the side of the stage and watch. From within the tank four "lead fish" come to the front of the stage and sing the opening segment of "Neglect". After they sing the refrain, the dance sequence begins, as other fish come out of the tank and join in. All of the fish come to the front of the stage and sing the final refrain. Curtain falls. End of Act I.

INTERMISSION

During the Intermission there can be a table set up in the lobby with literature about the project. Literature can include information on any organizations working in cooperation on the benefit. Copies of the Convention on the Rights of the Child can be included. Boxes or baskets can be set up to receive additional donations. CDs may be sold, or other items selected by the project committee such as a bake sale, etc. Art work prepared by the children can be displayed in the lobby.

ACT II

Scene 1

The curtain opens and the Dream Show Host and Dream Kids sing the reprise of the Dream Show song. At the end of the song one of the children walks to the front of the stage and takes a lead, expressing dissent that the situation with the hungry fish isn't really funny, and asks the group if they have ever felt helpless. Lights go down and the song "Poverty" begins.

Scene 2

During the song "Poverty" a multi-media presentation takes place. A slide show which is prepared in advance shows photographs of the children in the cast, interwoven with photographs of children in the country or countries they have chosen to help. While the alternating photos are shown, a pre-recorded tape of interviews with the children in the cast is played. In preparing the interviews, an adult project leader converses with each of the children about the topic of hunger, the facts they have learned, and the situations of children around the world. It is in this most sensitive segment of the musical that the children have an opportunity to express their feelings about the subject. At the end of the piece, one at a time the cast members go to stand beside and sing with the lead soloist, adding one child at a time to the line "can we give them more?"

Scene 3

The Dream Show Host re-appears and again congratulates the children on having asked the right question. The children are losing patience with this game, and tell him they want answers. With a flick of his wrist he "freezes" them, asks them what they would like to know, and exits. The children then converse, piecing together between themselves where they had been before they were all together in this dream, remembering back to watching T.V., reading magazines, and listening to the radio. They remember having all asked the question "Is there anything we can do?" They sing together quietly (this can be a cappella) "Help Them Live" as they slowly exit.

ACT III

Scene 1

The Dream Show Host is central onstage riding on a satellite. To his right, on the planet, there is a group of children representing children in North America. To his left there is a group of children representing the foreign country or countries on a different continent, such as Africa. The Dream Kids enter. One of the children trips and falls. On the other side of the stage a child says "Ouch!" The Dream Kids wonder how somebody on the other side of the world could feel what somebody on this side of the world feels. This core understanding of empathy leads into the song, "Everybody's Everybody".

During the song there is a dance, choreographed as if the children are dancing around the planet, all connected. The Dream Show Host lowers telephones on extended curly wires from the satellite down to the children. The telephone wires become part of the dance. All of the children in the cast sing the final verse of the song, and invite the audience to sing with them at the end.

When the song is over, the Dream Kids gather to make three phone calls to the children on the other continent. They ask: "Is there anything we can do?"

The children on the other end say "Send us some food". Another group calls and asks, "Is there anything we can do?" and the children answer, "Send us some doctors and medicine". The third group calls and asks, "Is there anything we can do?" and the children reply, "Tell them to wake up!"

As they sing the song, "We're Calling You", all of the children on the stage are holding phone receivers and the satellite is lit up. Leaving their phones on the stage, Group B, (the children from the other continent) walk down the center isle to the rear of the auditorium. When they get to the back, they begin singing "We Can Make a Difference", which is sung antiphonally between the two groups. This is the end of the show. Group B can go back up the isle to the stage for applause. The Dream Show Host invites the audience to join the children from the cast in the lobby.

CASTING THE ADULT SUPPORT TEAM

The suggested time line for producing Everybody's Everybody is 8 to 12 weeks. Time commitment will vary according to the skills of the children and professional or volunteers staff. If the musical is produced by a school or performing arts group, the roles listed below would be filled by staff people. If produced at an after school center or an under-staffed site, it is recommended that the Project Director seek out skilled volunteers. Ideally, all of these roles would be filled by different individuals.

Project Director:

The Project Director acts as a liaison between the organizations involved, the adults involved, and to oversee the project from beginning to end.

Publicist:

Writes and distributes press releases; Identifies local radio and/or TV stations who are willing to make free public service announcements; Sends out e-mail announcements; Organizes distribution of flyers and posters.

Dramatic Director:

Teaches roles, directs staging and overall presentation.

Music Director:

Teaches songs to actors and chorus; Prepares live musicians if available; Trains live percussion group to play over CD.

Choreographer:

Creates movements for Hunger, Neglect, Everybody's Everybody; Instructs and rehearses dances with children.

Multi-Media Coordinator:

Photographs children and art work; Seeks and finds authorized images of children in Africa; Makes and arranges slides; Operates slide projector at performance.

Art Director:

Prepares art work for bulletin board and slides ; Prepares flyers and posters with students; Coordinates with publicist; Works with children on preparing home-made costumes and images to be project as scenery.

Costume Coordinator:

Helps with designing and making costumes; Helps children with costumes back stage during performance.

Tech Crew:

Manages stage lights and sound system.

Stage Crew:

Helps with props and scene changes.

PREPARING THE PLAY

ACT I, Scenes 1, 2, and 3

Step 1: Research facts about places in the world where children are hungry and how they are affected by malnutrition. If a computer is available, it is a great resource for finding facts. An additional resource is the State of the World's Children Report , published annually by UNICEF. This document is available on-line:
http://www.unicef.org/sowc/

If no computer is available, research facts in available books, newspapers, magazines and local libraries

Step 2: Read the Convention on the Rights of the Child booklet included with this publication. **Identify which articles pertain** to the topics. Pass it around the group so that all become acquainted.

Step 3: A Creative Writing Exercise
Prepare a script to be read by a T.V. and a radio news announcer, telling facts about children in the world who suffer from malnutrition. For example "We interrupt this program to bring you a special message about the state of the world's children".

Step 4: Practice dramatization of the script, pretending to be a T.V. or radio news announcer. Take turns performing for other children.

Step 5: Select articles from magazines and newspapers pertaining to the topic. **Write articles, choose headlines, collect pictures.**

Step 6: Casting Scenes 1,2 and 3
Decide which children will be best cast for the T.V. announcer, radio announcer, and Fact Reporters #1, 2, and 3.

Step 7: Create a Bulletin Board

INTERMISSION

During the Intermission there can be a table set up in the lobby with literature about the project. Literature can include information on any organizations working in cooperation on the benefit. Copies of the Convention on the Rights of the Child can be made available. Boxes or baskets can be set up to receive additional donations. CDs may be sold, or other items selected by the project committee such as a bake sale, etc. Art work prepared by the children can be displayed in the lobby. Many online organizations provide posters.

ACT II, Scene 2

MULTI-MEDIA PRESENTATION

VISUAL MEDIA

Step 1: Collect photographs
- Collect photographs of the children who are in the cast. Prepare slides.
- Collect photographs of children in the selected country to be benefited by the production. For example, if the country is Sudan, find newspaper or magazine articles, or download photos from internet research. Contact local media for possible support on photographs.

Step 2: Create a slide presentation
- Place the slides in a carousel prior to the show. Alternate the photos of the children in the cast with the collected photos of children in the selected country.

Step 3: Practice
- The presentation of the slides should be ongoing during the length of the soundtrack to the song, "Poverty", and the interviews.

SOUND MEDIA

Step 1: Conduct interviews

In between verse 2 and 3 of the song, "Poverty", during the slide show, interviews with the children in the cast become the spoken text over the instrumental music. These may take place in one of three ways:

Option 1: Prerecorded *(requires sound engineer)*
Prior to the show, an adult spends quality time interviewing each child who is a member of the cast. The interviews may be tape recorded, compiled, and edited, and played during the slide show*.

Option 2: Live interviews *(requires separate advance rehearsal)*
During the slide show, assigned children become interviewers and interviews at a microphone. The interviewers ask questions.

Option 3: Panel Discussion *(requires separate advance rehearsal)*
If there is room on the stage, this scene could be set up as a panel discussion led by one qualified cast member, imitating the type of panel discussions often shown on television news programs.

The key topic of questions asked by the interviewer is the heart of the project itself. Discussion can include the information about children in other parts of the world, the information about hungry children in any circumstances, information about the Convention on the Rights of the Child, and how each child feels in relationship to these concerns. Emotional authenticity is encouraged.

*A loan copy of the original cast interviews is available through the publisher.

Everybody's Everybody

Script

Everybody's Everybody

ACT I:

Scene 1

Place:	A living room in an American home. Three children are watching television.
Time:	Evening
Characters:	T.V. Announcer, Children # 1,2,and 3, Mom #1
	As curtain opens, T.V. announcer is speaking (previously written script)

Child #1: What is a famine?

Child #2: That's when people are starving

Child #1: What country are we watching?

Child #3: Someplace in Africa.

Child #1: Why are people starving?

Child #2: Because……

Child #3: Yea, because…..

Child #1: *(yelling to next room)*: Mom, why are those children starving?

Mom #1: I don't know. Hey kids, it's bedtime, go to sleep.

Child #1: I don't understand.

BLACKOUT

Everybody's Everybody

ACT I:

Scene 2

Place:	A living room in a different home in America.. Dad sits in a chair reading the newspaper. Four children are reading magazines sitting on the floor on rug.
Time:	Evening
Characters:	Children #4,#5,#6,#7, Dad

Child #4:   Look at this!

Child #5:   Woe……

Other children go to look, gathering around the magazine

Child #6:   What is it?

Child #4:   I think it's a kid

Child #7:   That's a kid?

Child #4:   *(takes the picture to her dad)* Dad, look at this picture. What's going on with this kid?

Dad: He's starving

Child #7:   Let's go give him some food

Child #5:   Yea, he can have my broccoli!

Dad: He's too far away

Child #5:   Not for the space shuttle…..

BLACKOUT

Everybody's Everybody

ACT I:

Scene 3

Place:	a child's bedroom….a boom box is playing music
Time:	evening
Characters:	Child #8, Mom #2, Radio Announcer
	As scene begins, Child #8 is dancing to the music coming from the boom box

Mom #2: Turn off the music please, it's bedtime.

Child #8: OK mom..

Radio Announcer: *(previously written script)*…newsflash…..

Child #8: Mama! Mama!

Mom #2: What is it?

Child #8: Thousands of children died today...

Mom #2: How? What happened?

Child #8: People are starving in *(name of country)*

Mom #2: Oh, the famine. Now, turn off the radio and go to sleep. You have school tomorrow.

Child #8: But, Mom………

Mom #2: Go to bed!

BLACKOUT

Everybody's Everybody

ACT I :

Scene 4

Place:	During the BLACKOUT this scene takes place in the dark as the chorus sings "Help Them Live"
Time:	The children from scenes 1, 2, and 3 have gone to sleep and are in transit to a dream where they will all meet up
Characters:	Children # 1, 2, 3, 4, 5, 6, 7, 8, Chorus, Fact Reporters #1, #2, #3

SONG: HELP THEM LIVE
VERSE 1, 2 and 3:

VERSE 1:   DID YOU HEAR ABOUT THE CHILD WHO DIED?
Children 1-8:   DID YOU HEAR ABOUT THE CHILD WHO CRIED?
                   DID YOU HEAR? DID YOU SEE?
                   DID YOU FEEL SOMETHING MOVE INSIDE?
                   IS THERE ANYTHING WE CAN DO?
                   IS THERE ANYTHING WE CAN GIVE?
                   IS THERE ANYWAY WE CAN HELP THE CHILDREN LIVE?
                   HELP THEM LIVE, HELP THEM LIVE,
                   HELP THEM LIVE, HELP THEM LIVE.

VERSE 2:   *Chorus members join in with children #1-8*

BRIDGE:

During the instrumental bridge, a spotlight appears on each of the Three Fact Reporters consecutively. Fact Reporter #1 and #2 speak facts about the state of the worlds children. Fact Reporter #3 speaks a selected Article from the Convention on the Rights of the Child.

VERSE 3:   *Project the lyrics on a screen or wall*

Fact Reporter: *Gesture an invitation to the audience to sing.*

BLACKOUT

Everybody's Everybody

ACT I:

Scene 5

Place:	In a dream, a television game-show, called the "Dream Show"
Time:	During the night when the children from scenes 1, 2, and 3 are sleeping
Characters:	Children #1-8, Dream Show Host, Hunger Monster
	Music begins as scene opens. Lights up.

SONG: DREAM SHOW

Host:	WELCOME TO THE DREAM SHOW!
Children:	WHAT IS THE DREAM SHOW?
Host: *(to audience)*	WELCOME TO THE DREAM SHOW!
Children:	WHAT IS THE DREAM SHOW?
Host:	WHAT WAS THE QUESTION? SHALL WE ASK?
	WHERE WOULD WE LIKE TO GO?
	WHAT WAS THE QUESTION? SHALL WE ASK?
	WHAT WOULD WE LIKE TO KNOW?
Children:	WHAT WILL THE DREAM SHOW SHOW?
Host:	WHAT WILL THE DREAM SHOW SHOW?
	THAT THE GOAL OF THIS GAME IS TO
	ASK THE RIGHT QUESTION!
Children:	WHAT'S THE RIGHT QUESTION?
Host:	ASK THE RIGHT QUESTION!
Children:	WHAT'S THE RIGHT QUESTION?

(Repeat entire song one time)

Enter, Hunger Monster

Host: *(looking scared)* We'll be right back after a word from our sponsor…..

Attacca "HUNGER"

Everybody's Everybody

ACT I :

Scene 5 (continued)

SONG: HUNGER

Hunger Monster:
VERSE 1- 2:
    I AM HUNGER
    I AM KNOCKING AT YOUR DOOR
    I AM HUNGER
    I AM VISITING THE POOR
    PEOPLE HUNGER BECAUSE THEY HAVE NO GRAIN
    PLANTS HAVE HUNGER WHEN THERE IS NO RAIN

    REPEAT, adding dance to VERSE 2

VERSE 3
Hunger Monster:	I AM HUNGER
Children:	IS THERE ANYTHING WE CAN DO?
Hunger Monster:	I AM KNOCKING AT YOUR DOOR
Children:	IS THERE ANYTHING WE CAN GIVE?
Hunger Monster:	I AM HUNGER
Children:	IS THERE ANYWAY WE CAN HELP THE CHILDREN LIVE?
	HELP THEM LIVE, HELP THEM LIVE,
	HELP THEM LIVE, HELP THEM LIVE.

Exit Hunger Monster
Enter Dream Show Host

Host :   Very good, very good! (he claps for the children)
    You have asked the right question. Now, what is the prize?

An unseen announcer
speaks from offstage: Congratulations! You have just won a brand new brand of an age old, long forgotten fish tank. This tank comes completely equipped with a fresh array of frustrated but still determined tropical fish. Looking closely we can see that the fish have been, oh, they haven't been fed….For your bonus prize, a stale can of urgently needed, potentially life-saving government surplus fish food!

Child #2   Why are these fish starving?

Host :   They haven't been fed.

Child #2 :   Why haven't they been fed?

Host :   Good question! Observe…….

Everybody's Everybody

ACT I:

Scene 6

SONG: NEGLECT

Fish One:	FOR SEVEN LONG YEARS WE'VE BEEN SWIMMING IN THIS TANK
Fish Two:	WATCHING THE PARADE GO BY
Fish Three:	HOPING TO CATCH THE EYE
Fish Four:	OF ANYBODY OUT THERE
#1:	BUT WE'RE JUST FISH, THEY DON'T CARE ABOUT US
#1 & 2:	BUT WE'RE JUST FISH, THEY DON'T CARE ABOUT US
#1,2, & 3:	BUT WE'RE JUST FISH, THEY DON'T CARE ABOUT US
#1,2,3, & 4:	BUT WE'RE JUST FISH, THEY DON'T CARE ABOUT US
Fish One:	FOR SEVEN LONG YEARS WE'VE BEEN STARING AT THAT CAN
Fish Two:	WAITING FOR THE MAN WHO SEES
Fish Three:	HUNGER IS A SOCIAL DISEASE
Fish Four:	OF EVERYBODY IN HERE
#1:	BUT WE'RE JUST FISH, THEY DON'T CARE ABOUT US
#1 & 2:	WE'RE JUST FISH, THEY DON'T CARE ABOUT US
#1,2 & 3:	WE'RE JUST FISH, THEY DON'T CARE ABOUT US
#1,2,3 & 4:	WE'RE JUST FISH, THEY DON'T CARE ABOUT US
All Fish:	WHEN WE FORGET TO SHOW THIS WORLD OUR LOVING
	WHEN WE FORGET TO SHOW THIS WORLD RESPECT
	WHEN WE FORGET THE VALUE OF ANOTHER HUMAN BEING
	WE BECOME THE VICTIMS OF NEGLECT
	NEGLECT WILL CREEP UP ON WHEN YOU'RE NOT REALLY LOOKING
	NEGLECT WILL CREEP UP ON WHEN YOU DON'T REALLY CARE
	NEGLECT WILL CREEP UP ON WHEN YOU'RE NOT REALLY LISTENING TO
	THE OTHER PEOPLE NEEDING YOU IN THE WORLD OUT THERE

(Tune continues as instrumental, fish do break dancing, Dream Kids join in on dancing. After dance, vocal is repeated.)

END OF ACT I,   CURTAIN CLOSES,   INTERMISSION

Everybody's Everybody

ACT II :

Scene 1

> *Lights come up, children from Act I are sitting in a circle.*
>
> Place: A dream.
>
> Time: Daytime an American TV game show.
>
> Characters: Child One, Child Two, Child Three, Child Five, Child Four, Child Six, Child Seven, Child Eight, Dream Show Host.

Enter Host.

SONG: DREAM SHOW (REPRISE)

Host: WELCOME TO THE DREAM SHOW!

Kids: WHAT IS THE DREAM SHOW?

Host: WELCOME TO THE DREAM SHOW!

Kids: WHAT IS THE DREAM *SHOW?*

Host: *WHAT WAS THE QUESTION? SHALL WE ASK?*
WHERE WOULD WE LIKE TO GO?
WHAT WAS THE QUESTION? SHALL WE ASK?
WHAT WOULD WE LIKE TO KNOW?

Kids: WHAT WILL THE DREAM SHOW SHOW?

Host: (SPOKEN) WHAT WILL THE DREAM SHOW SHOW?
THAT THE GOAL OF THIS GAME IS TO ASK THE RIGHT QUESTION!

Kids: *WHAT'S THE RIGHT QUESTION?*

Host: *ASK THE RIGHT QUESTION!*

Kids: *WHAT'S THE RIGHT QUESTION?*

Host: *ASK THE RIGHT QUESTION!*
Kids: WHAT'S THE RIGHT QUESTION?

(While kids sing, Child #3 walks to front stage across from looking at odds)

Child #3:   Do you really think this is fun?
Do you really think those fish are happy living that way?
Have you ever felt helpless?

Everybody's Everybody

ACT II :

Scene 2

Place:	This scene is visually a multi-media slide show during which the song "Poverty" is sung and interviews are the spoken text (see previous page regarding options)
Time :	Although this scene is still within context of the children's dream, it has more of the quality of "reality" than previous dream scenes.
Characters :	Verses 1, 2, and 3 of "Poverty" are sung as a solo by Child #3 of the Dream Kids. The interviews can involve any of the cast members selected for this scene. At the end of the song, on the line "Can we give them more?" the soloist singing is joined on each repetition of that line by one more child joining in and forming a gradual line.

SONG: POVERTY

VERSE 1:	NOT ENOUGH TO GO AROUND
Child #3 Solo:	STICKS AND PEBBLES ON THE GROUND
	POVERTY, NOTHING TO BE FOUND
VERSE 2:	EMPTY SPACES, BARREN LANDS
	HUNGRY FACES, SCHRIVELING HANDS
	POVERTY, NO ONE UNDERSTANDS.

BEGIN VISUAL MEDIA & INTERVIEWS
REFER TO *"Preparing for Act II Scene 2"*

VERSE 3:	WHO ARE WE IF WE IGNORE
	THE HELPLESS CRYING OF THE POOR
	POVERTY CAN WE GIVE THEM MORE?
Child #4:	CAN WE GIVE THEM MORE?
Child #5:	CAN WE GIVE THEM MORE?
Child #6:	CAN WE GIVE THEM MORE?
Child #7:	CAN WE GIVE THEM MORE?
Child #8:	CAN WE GIVE THEM MORE?
Child #1:	CAN WE GIVE THEM MORE?
Child #2:	CAN WE GIVE THEM MORE?
Child #8:	I think they would say "Thank-you"

Everybody's Everybody

ACT II :

Scene 3

Place:	In the dream
Time:	continuation of the dream
Characters:	Children # 1-8, Dream Show Host

Enter Host

Host: Very good! Very good! We're getting very good at this.
We've been asking the right question!
And now, for the PRIZE…

Child # 2: We're sick and tired of your stupid game.

Child # 8: Yea! And your prizes aren't so hot anyway.

Child # 4: We didn't come here to play games.

Child # 5: Questions!
All your questions just lead to more questions.
We want ANSWERS. NOW!

All: Yea! We want answers now!

Host freezes them with hand gestures.

Host: What was the question?
What did we ask?
What is that long ago?
What was the question?
What brings us here?
What would we like to know?

Why did we come here?
Why did we ask?
What would we like to know?

Exit Host

Everybody's Everybody

ACT II :

Scene 3 continued

Child # 5:	He did it again!
Child # 6:	How did we get here in the first place?
Child # 8:	Where did you come from?
Child # 4:	We were reading the newspaper.
Child # 1:	We were watching T.V.
Child # 8:	I was listening to the radio.

"HELP THEM LIVE MUSIC" begins

Child # 2: What was on the radio?
What was in the newspaper?
What was on TV?

All: The famine.

Child # 2: We all asked a question …

Voices from offstage: Did you hear?
Did you see?
Did you feel something move inside?
Is there anything we can do?
Is there anything we can give?
Is there anyway we can help the children live?

Dream kids sing refrain while exiting. (Stage right)
"Help them live" music continues, fade out

Everybody's Everybody

ACT III :

Scene 1

Place:	Image of planet earth in the sky, satellite in the atmosphere connecting continents
Time:	This is a continuation of the dream
Characters:	Children # 1-8, Dream Show Host, Group A: Children in America, Group B: Children on a different continent, *(Africa)* dancers in the dance sequence, entire cast

Enter Dream kids

Child # 8 falls

Children from Africa shout: OUCH!

Child # 4: Are you all right?

Child # 8: Its O.K. just a scratch

Child # 5: Who said OUCH?

Child # 8: What the heck's going on there?

Child # 5: How could somebody over there feel what he felt?

Child # 4: I understand.

SONG: EVERYBODY'S EVERYBODY

Everybody's Everybody

ACT III :

Scene 1 continued

SONG: EVERYBODY'S EVERYBODY

VERSE 1:
Child #4 Solo: THERE'S A PLACE WHERE OTHER'S TEARS ARE MY TEARS
THERE'S PLACE WHERE OTHER'S DREAMS ARE MINE
AND ANY CHILD WHO NEEDS YOU
COULD BE THE CHILD WHO LEADS YOU TO THAT PLACE
WHERE EVERYBODY'S EVERYBODY, EVERYBODY'S EVERYBODY,
EVERYBODY'S EVERYBODY…

VERSE 2:
Child #3 Solo: THERE'S A PLACE WHERE OTHER'S SONGS ARE MY SONGS
THERE'S A PLACE WHERE OTHER'S EARS ARE MINE
AND ANY CHILD WHO NEEDS YOU
COULD BE THE CHILD WHO LEADS YOU TO THAT PLACE,
WHERE EVERYBODY'S EVERYBODY, EVERYBODY'S EVERYBODY,
EVERYBODY'S EVERYBODY…

BRIDGE: WHEN YOU THINK YOU'RE ALL ALONE
AND NOBODY CAN HEAR YOU
THE ATMOSPHERE IS TELEPHONE
AND EVERYBODY'S NEAR YOU

VERSE 3:
Entire cast: THERE'S A PLACE WHERE OTHER'S HANDS ARE MY HANDS
THERE'S PLACE WHERE OTHER'S HEARTS ARE MINE
AND ANY CHILD WHO NEEDS YOU
COULD BE THE CHILD WHO LEADS YOU TO THAT PLACE
WHERE EVERYBODY'S EVERYBODY, EVERYBODY'S EVERYBODY,
EVERYBODY'S EVERYBODY…

Dance sequence, 26 measures

REPEAT VERSE 3

Children invite the audience to sing with them. Chorus and dance may continue until the end of the music.

Everybody's Everybody

ACT III :

Scene 1 continued

Three children in group A make three phone calls, reaching three children in group B

Child from group A:	Hi! I'm (child says name) calling from (place). Is there anything we can do?
Child from group B:	Can you send us some food?
Child from group A:	Hi! I'm (child says name) calling from (place). Is there anything we can do?
Child from group B:	Can you please send us some doctors and medicine
Child from group A:	Hi! I'm (child says name) calling from (place). Is there anything we can do?
Child from group B:	Tell them to wake up!
Child from group A:	Tell them what?
Child from group B:	*(Other children join in)* Tell them to wake up!
Child from group A:	Tell them what?
Children from group B:	Tell them to wake up!

SONG: WE'RE CALLING YOU

Everybody's Everybody

ACT III :

Scene 1 continued

SONG: WE'RE CALLING YOU

Group B: SLEEPERS AWAKE, MAKE NO MISTAKE
THIS ISN'T A DREAM AT ALL
LISTEN AND HEAR, SO DISTANT SO NEAR
THE CHILDREN HAVE MADE A CALL

(The satellite lights up– all children have phone receivers)

CHORUS: WE'RE CALLING YOU. WE'RE CALLING YOU.
WE'RE CALLING YOU. WE'RE CALLING YOU.

REPEAT SONG:

*Chorus sings in two parts.
Group B walks out through the aisles towards back of auditorium while singing. When Group B reaches the back of the auditorium then Attacca "We Can Make A Difference:"*

Everybody's Everybody

ACT III :

Scene 1 continued

SONG: WE CAN MAKE A DIFFERENCE

Group B:	WE CAN MAKE A DIFFERENCE
Group A :	WE CAN MAKE A DIFFERENCE
Group B:	WE CAN MAKE A DIFFERENCE
Group A:	WE CAN MAKE A DIFFERENCE
Group B:	WE CAN MAKE A DIFFERENCE
Group A :	WE CAN MAKE A DIFFERENCE
Group B:	WE CAN MAKE A DIFFERENCE
Group A:	WE CAN MAKE A DIFFERENCE
All:	WE CAN MAKE A DIFFERENCE
All:	STARTING FROM WHERE WE ARE,
	WE CAN REACH PEOPLE FAR AWAY.
	STARTING WITH WHAT WE KNOW,
	WE'RE GONNA HELP TO SHOW THE WAY!
Group B:	WE CAN MAKE A DIFFERENCE
Group A :	WE CAN MAKE A DIFFERENCE
Group B:	WE CAN MAKE A DIFFERENCE
Group A:	WE CAN MAKE A DIFFERENCE
Group B:	WE CAN MAKE A DIFFERENCE
Group A :	WE CAN MAKE A DIFFERENCE
Group B:	WE CAN MAKE A DIFFERENCE
Group A:	WE CAN MAKE A DIFFERENCE
All:	WE CAN MAKE A DIFFERENCE
	YES!

During Instrumental Interlude the Dream Show Host invites the audience to join the cast in the lobby.

REPEAT SONG: *Group A Exits down center isle during repeat. Final word YES! is sung by entire cast from back of auditorium.*

(CURTAIN)

Everybody's Everybody

Scores

- Help them Live
- Dream Show
- Hunger
- Neglect
- Dream Show (reprise)
- Poverty
- Everybody's Everybody
- We're Calling You
- We Can Make A Difference

Help Them Live

Everybody's Everybody

Dream Show Theme Song

© Merrill Collins 1985   www.spiralingmusic.com   Published by Spiraling Music Company ASCAP

Everybody's Everybody

Neglect

Cue: Scene is ready with enlarged fish tank.

© Merrill Collins 1985   www.spiralingmusic.com   Published by Spiraling Music Company ASCAP

Everybody's Everybody

Cue: *I understand.*

© Merrill Collins 1985 www.spiralingmusic.com Published by Spiraling Music Company ASCAP

Appendicies

Notes for Music Educators

The Everybody's Everybody soundtrack can be a great introduction to world music. The special sounds you hear include rain stick, tibetan bell, congas, jimbe, dumbec, tabla, and bonsurai flute. If your group performs to the prerecorded soundtrack, live percussion instruments may be added. Acquire or make rainsticks, bells, etc., or experiment with instruments you have available.

If you have capable group of instrumentalists and choose to perform the soundtrack live, include intercultural sounds to broaden the learning experience.

Congas

Tabla

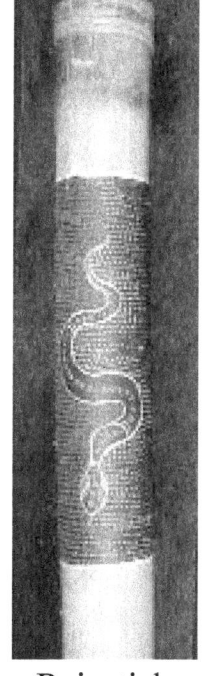
Rainstick

Talking Drum

Bongos

How to use the Instrumental Soundtrack

Use as a soundtrack
For rehearsals and a live performance, use the CD or a streaming track through a PA system or appropriateley sized speaker/system. Mic the singers and do a sound-check on the volume balance.

Use with multimedia
Rip the track you want to use from the CD to your hard drive, and open with your multimedia editing program.

Background Listening
Use the recorded instrumental music for background listening while are working on other aspects of the project. This not only helps to relax and focus on work, it helps performers get to know the music, visualize themselves ahead of time and commit their parts to memory.

Special Instructions for Non-Musicians:

A few basic rhythm terms:
- **a beat** = a basic unit of rhythm; a pulse.
- **a measure** = a group of beats within two bar-lines
- **time signature** = the numbers at the beginning of the score. The top number shows how many beats are in each measure.
    Example: 4 indicates 4 beats per measure.
                    4

How to count the introductions of songs:
Count with movement of feet, fingers, hands, or with additional live percussion. On each score, the numbers tell how many measures of introductory music lead up to the place where the singing starts; also how many measures are in interludes.

How to find the Pitch

Every score indicates the key in which a song is written and the first note. Using the image (below), go to a piano keyboard and find the first note. Hum along with it. Then start the CD.

Key to Songs in the Musical:

Song	Starting Pitch
Help Them Live	G♭
Dream Show	G
Hunger	E
Neglect *(refrain)*	D♭
Poverty	B
Everybody's Everybody	G#
We're Calling You	A♭
We Can Make a Difference	D#

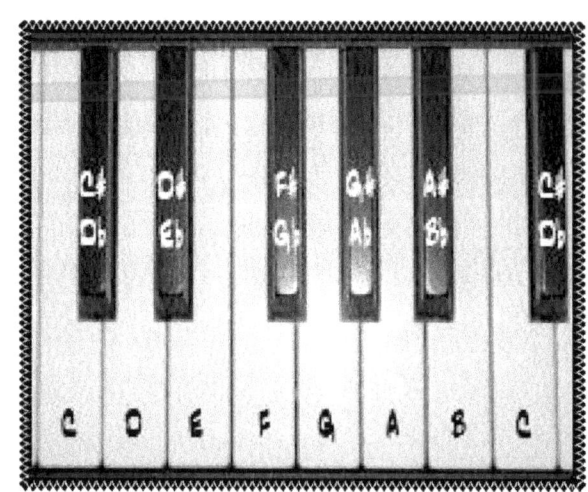

46

RESOURCES

The following resources compliment these projects and can help raise awareness:

Convention on the Rights of the Child
Learn more about this important document at: unicef.org/child-rights-convention. The text can be downloaded at https://www.unicef.org/child-rights-convention/convention-text, and small purple booklets can be ordered inexpensively at https://hreusa.org/shop/

Human Rights Education Associates (HREA)
An international non-governmental organization that supports human rights learning; the training of activists and professionals; the development of educational materials and programming; and community-building through on-line technologies. www.hrea.org

Educators for Social Responsibility
Educators for Social Responsibility (ESR) helps educators work with young people to develop the social skills, emotional competencies, and qualities of character they need to succeed in school and become contributing members of their communities. http://www.esrnational.org

Earthdance
Earthdance, the Global Dance Festival for Peace has grown to become the world's largest simultaneous music and dance event. Founded in 1997, with 22 cities and 18 countries participating, Earthdance has now expanded to over 240 cities in 50 countries, with locations ranging from the club-lands of New York to the rainforests of Brazil. Every year, in alignment with the International Day of Peace, over 200,000 people unite in dance with hundreds of thousands more joining online in support of global peace and humanitarian aims.
www.earthdance.org

Two good websites for researching and supporting current hunger issues are:

The State of the World's Children
UNICEF's annual report on the children worldwide is a full-color book with photographs, art, and statistics that is very useful for research. Order from your local bookseller or access online at: www.unicef.org/reports/state-of-worlds-children

and

United Nations World Food Program
This organization brings life-saving relief in emergencies and use food assistance to build peace, stability and prosperity for people recovering from conflict, disasters and the impact of climate change. www.wfp.org, www.wfpusa.org

ABOUT THE ARTISTS

Merrill Collins, *keyboards, rainstick, bells* • Pope Flyne, *talking drum, congas, djembe* • Joseph Hebert, *'cello* • Chris Ray Collins, *bongos, djembe, dumbec* • Charles Moselle, *bonsurai flute, silver flute, saxophones, dijiri-do, congas* • Tim Witter, *tablas*

Engineering: Charles Moselle • Mastering: Bryan Matteson, Skyline Studios • Graphic design: Kristen Caven & Fatima Yousuf
Cover Photography: Yvon Chausseblanche • Score design: Karl Pister.

Tim Witter with tablas

Chris Ray Collins with dumbec

Pope Flyne with talking drum

ABOUT THE COMPOSER

Merrill Collins began writing and performing music in early childhood, with the encouragement of a family of artists, musicians and inventors. She earned her Master's Degree at the San Francisco Conservatory of Music on a full scholarship. Merrill's career has expanded from concert performances to multimedia pieces and educational humanitarian projects. While raising her son Chris Ray, Merrill created music and community service projects for Montessori schools, YMCA School Age Child Care programs, private, parochial and public schools. During the years 1986-1987 she held the title Composer-in-Residence of Pathways to Peace and her programs become the original curricula model for Children's Peace Education.

Merrill's experience in the field of drama includes choral direction of five award winning musicals at Bishop O'Dowd High School, coach-accompanist at A.C.T., and seventeen years as senior musician in the department of Theatre, Dance and Performance Studies at the University of California, Berkeley.

Through her music, Merrill's heartfelt voice for global harmony and humanist evolution has touched thousands of listeners around the world. She has produced performances of original music for many major events and broadcasts, including the 50th Anniversary of the United Nations (1995), Airlift to Africa (1986), In Concert Against Aids (1989), Human Rights Day (1987), World Habitat Day (1988); and anniversary concerts for Amnesty International and The United Way. Other major performances include "Licht ins Dunkel" (1991, Austria), "Terra Vitae" (1992, Berkeley), and "The Web" (1996, Berkeley). She performed at the World Religions conference in Cape town, South Africa in December, 1999, where her works were cited as "Gifts of Service to the World."

Merrill cooking something up

Currently Merrill produces music, performs, and presents on the home front and at international conferences. Workshops on this material are available to educators, child care programs, and community organizations seeking to develop intercultural relationships.

www.ingramcontent.com/pod-product-compliance
Lightning Source LLC
Chambersburg PA
CBHW061823290426
44110CB00027B/2958